Design by Katie Benezra

ISBN 978-1-4197-3222-5

Printed and bound in China
10 9 8 7 6 5 4 3 2

Abrams Noterie products are available at special discounts
when purchased in quantity for premiums and promotions
as well as fundraising or educational use. Special editions
can also be created to specification. For details, contact
specialsales@abramsbooks.com or the address below.

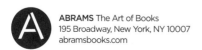

ABRAMS The Art of Books
195 Broadway, New York, NY 10007
abramsbooks.com